RMS

2nd ~~Low to offset filter~~
Limiter

3rd Equalization

Pearl Button Press

Don't Quit Your Daydream

First published March 2018 by Pearl Button Press

Harvey, Ray
Don't Quit Your Daydream
p. cm.
ISBN 9781980521174
Copyright © April 2018

Pearl Button Press
305 W. Magnolia Street #162
Fort Collins CO 80521

Contents

Don't Quit Your Daydream

How to drop out of school, fire your boss, and change the world

Ray Harvey

To Hell With Swords and Garter

Did you feel that tug?

Like a half-forgotten idea you can't *quite* put out of your head — the escalating sensation in the center of your chest telling you it's time to shift your life?

Nothing outrageous — no come-to-God moment, this — but rather a soft yet persistent pull in another direction: an urge, sourced somewhere deep within, impelling you to do that thing for which you were born:

Create.

Admit it. You often feel it swelling up and pulsing inside you.

And once you acknowledge it, it begins to intensify, struggling to take shape so that it might burst open at last, like a tarantula-firework, illuminating a dark world desperately in need.

Yet, at the same time, an oppositional force tugs at you too: the uncertainty and fear of breaking away from the pack, of leaving your staid but secure position, of running out of money, not making your bills, evicted, hungry, homeless.

And so you ignore the pull to create, and you do nothing about it.

You bury yourself back in the safety of your soul-sucking job.

Oh, you tinker with your passions, here and there. You become something of a hobbyist.

But, in the end, you evade and ignore your dreams, and you meanwhile drown yourself in booze or food or drugs or sex or whathaveyou. And you tell yourself that staying in your current lifestyle is the right thing to do.

Still, that irrepressible part of you can't be completely suppressed. It's like a little creative beastie pulsing with life and pushing and kicking to break open inside you, yearning to grow.

Have you ever watched the slow, silent death of a thing?

Have you witnessed the life-force leaking out of a living organism, bit-by-bit, and gradually draining that organism of all its beautiful vitality, until one day, one hour, one minute, one second, the organism is suddenly no longer alive?

It is wrenching to see.

It is also ominously familiar.

And yet, and yet …

And yet what you always hear about pursuing your dreams and if you do everything will work out — this *is*, to a certain extent, a lot of nonsense.

You *can* run out of money.

You *can* get evicted.

You *can* go hungry.

Your life, in short, can nose-dive.

I've been there.

It is not pleasant: showering at the beach, brushing your teeth in the bathrooms of all-night convenient stores or laundromats, unable to write because you can't concentrate, because you're so worried about what's going to happen to you.

And so knowing this is possible, what do you do?

You tell yourself you're being prudent after all. You're being sensible, practical.

You tell yourself that you need to first do this and then that and then you need to go back to college and then you need to do this other thing, and *then,* perhaps — *perhaps* — you'll pursue your passion to become a creator, at last.

The truth is that you're stalling because you can't muster the courage to take the plunge.

You have the power within you *right now* to change everything for the better — and if you don't try, do you know what will happen?

You'll die without ever knowing what you could have done.

Am I telling you, then, to quit your life of safety and security?

Yes, I am.

I'm telling you that if the life you're living is stultifying you and preventing you from bringing forth that which is most vital within you, you should *indeed* quit your safe secure life.

I'm telling you to stop treating your passions as hobbies.

I'm telling you to stop glutting yourself on the things that drown out your dreams.

I'm telling you to start thinking of your passions and your dreams as your profession: your life-force, your reason for living.

Start today.

Start *now*.

You just have to do it.

Slash your expenses.

Plan it.

Map it out.

Focus your brain.

Find a freelance or part-time gig.

Construct a fall-back plan for when everything goes straight to hell, which it might.

Frightening?

Inexpressibly.

Difficult?

You bet your ass.

Every great achievement is difficult, and every path leading to it frightening.

We each live primarily inside of our own mind. Our lives are largely an attempt to give form to our psychological existence. We do that through what we create.

It's do or die:

Life is do or die.

So go and do.

And to hell with swords and garter — and anything else that strangles the creative beastie so desperately yearning to hatch open and take shape inside of you.

How Good Do You Want to Be?

Does it keep you awake at night?

Do you burn in a white-hot fever?

Make it hotter, baby.

Stoke it.

Let it burn.

***

Because it's as you always suspected:

You are *not* the product of your genetic code, and nobody is genetically doomed to mediocrity.

In actuality, it's the opposite of what you've always been told. Your life is yours to shape and mold.

Genes are not blueprints dictating precisely what you become.

Your genes are only one of countless components, in a complex interplay of components, that go into the making of an almost infinitely complicated organism, the sum total of which is determined fundamentally by your desire:

Your will to become the person you most want to become is the main factor in determining your future.

The drive to persist even in the face of overwhelming odds comes chiefly from within.

So I ask again:

How good do you want to be?

That desire is far more important than your pedigree.

***

Brandon Mroz is the first ice skater in human history to complete, in sanctioned competition, a jump called a quadruple Lutz. He did this on November 12, 2011, at the ripe age of twenty-one.

Perfecting this jump requires untold hours and days and weeks and years of practice, and much of that time Brandon spent falling down on the cold, ungiving ice.

He began skating when he was three-and-a-half years old, and he performed his first successful quadruple Lutz — non-sanctioned — in 2010. A cursory calculation tells us that in his lifetime of practicing, he fell approximately thirty thousand times before landing a successful quadruple Lutz.

Yet those thirty-thousand spills were not in vain: through them, he *became* excellent. He raised the standard and in so doing he changed a certain sector of the world.

This story — the story of falling on your ass thousands of times and getting back up, over and over again to master a skill, of spending your time in this way — it is in many ways the perfect metaphor because it goes to the very essence of where human excellence originates, in *any* endeavor:

Falling down thousands upon thousands of times and getting back up and practicing it again and again — day in day out, week in week out, year in year out — *that* is how people learn to master a given skill.

That is how women and men of every stripe and variety achieve great things.

It is how humans grow wings.

***

It also raises a profound and inevitable question:

Why would anyone put him or herself through so much falling for a reward that looms so far into the future and the success of which is hardly assured?

Why, indeed?

Concerning exceptional achievement, it is, perhaps, the deepest inquiry that exists. And the more you think about it, the more you see that the inquiry is nearly bottomless, going so far down into the human psyche, beyond psychology, that it may well be that no one from the outside can penetrate it fully.

Why *do* people who become great pay the price they must pay in order to get there?

***

One thing we can clearly see:

People who achieve excellence *learn* to love the task they've chosen. They therefore focus almost exclusively upon the task.

It's a type of monomania, a singleminded and often obsessive focus.

In essence, people who become great say to themselves: how can I solve this specific problem?

They do not say: how will solving this problem benefit others or me?

Or:

What is the higher cause in solving this problem?

They instead focus laser-like upon the task itself.

When that task is taken care of, they move to the next task and focus upon it with the same intensity, and then move on, and so on.

***

The creator must be driven and must have focus. That focus *first* comes from within, but the most crucial point to recognize — and it is absolutely vital — is that neither the passion nor the focus start out fully formed.

Passion and focus, in other words, do not spring full-blown from the head of Zeus. They do not accompany us into the world like the parts of our body. They develop as our interest in the thing develops.

Which is why great performers, whether musicians or athletes, scientists or painters, writers or architects or anything else, start out as all of us do: learning things slowly and tediously, often when we're young, perhaps taking lessons that are more-or-less forced upon us.

The difference between the good and the great, the hobbyist and the expert, the mediocre and the excellent, is that at some point, people who become great *choose* to pursue the given activity and make it the focal point of their life.

The significance of this cannot be overstated.

As one jazz virtuoso explained it, describing the precise moment in childhood that her piano lessons ceased to be a chore:

"One day, when I was twelve or thirteen, after having taken [piano] lessons for years, I was struck in an almost epiphany-like fashion with the range of possibilities that lay before me. It seemed endless and at my fingertips, the potential for artistic expression inexhaustible. It was at that moment that I made my decision and ceased thinking of piano as a hobby."

Passion develops.

It does not emerge fully formed.

First we must endure the effort of early practice, and then we must decide if the activity is what we wish to pursue.

In this sense — a general sense — creativity represents the highest levels of human excellence.

This is true no matter the domain in which you work, no matter the subject.

***

Every single person born healthy has the power within to become extraordinary. And in the bud and blossom of life, everyone sees for herself or himself a big and bright and beautiful future.

To be exceptional, you must first forsake many things that are unexceptional — forsake the foolish and live: it is a corollary.

It's also, for most, the biggest obstacle.

***

Purpose and self-development are the aim of life.

Vice smothers self-development and purpose, and it can make the pull of mediocrity almost irresistibly strong.

Most won't overcome it, but it doesn't have to be that way. Mediocrity is not fated. It is accumulated.

The life you've always imagined for yourself is within your reach — it's yours to control — but reaching it requires a great deal of effort. That's why the overwhelming majority of people retreat into the relative safety of the group. Which group? Whichever one most represents the values any given person has accumulated over the years.

The way out of mediocrity isn't college.

The way out of mediocrity is to focus first upon the task — on developing knowledge.

The way out of mediocrity is the decision to *do,* and the willingness to fail. Because mistakes and failure are part of the process.

The first move, then, is in explicitly recognizing what things you genuinely like to do.

Happiness must ensue.

13:33

It's Not How Clever or How Smart You ARE It's How Clever and Smart You WANT to be

The most successful people in life aren't particularly gifted or talented.

They become successful, rather, by wanting to be successful.

Genetic giftedness is largely a figment.

There are really no such things as prodigies.

Talent is a process.

Have you ever noticed that the smartest kids in school are almost never the ones who go on to be the most successful in life?

School in its best state teaches datum, not ambition or desire or will — all of which things can be encouraged and fostered, but not really taught.

Ambition, desire, will, persistence — these, as you may or may not guess, are the greatest predictors of success.

***

No human being and no living thing begins her life by undercutting it.

No human being, no matter how pampered or abused, no matter how spoiled or mistreated, starts out by giving up or giving in.

No one starts life irrevocably defeated.

Abandoning the dreams of one's youth comes only after a protracted process of perversion.

The time it takes before this mindset dominates differs for each person.

For most it is a gradual accretion of pressures and set-backs and frustrations and small failures, or by the systematic inculcation of mantras that this life doesn't really matter, that our dreams can't be fully realized anyway, and that human existence is accidental or meaningless or both — only to find, one day, that their passion, once a glowing force within, is now gone … but where and how?

Others, having no depth of thought or will, stop at the first sign of adversity.

Only the truly passionate persist. Only the truly passionate retain for a lifetime the vision they had of themselves when they were young. Only a handful maintain for a lifetime the beautiful vision of their youth and go on to give it form.

The means by which we give that vision form is our work.

No matter what any given person may become — no matter how good, bad, ugly, or great — in the springtime of life, each person at one time believes that her existence is important, and that big wonderful things await.

Each and every single human being has the potential to retain that vision, and each and every single human being *should* retain that vision, because it is the true and correct vision.

College, I submit, can do irreversible damage to it.

***

Unactualized potential is a tragedy.

Nonconformity for nonconformity sake is meaningless.

Nonconformity for the sake of reason and independent thought, however, is a virtue.

Independent thought is a prerequisite of genius, and it takes courage to think for yourself.

Courage is also a virtue.

Blind conformity is the opposite of independent thought.

Ambition, too, is a virtue.

Virtue is human excellence. It is The Good.

The Good is that which fosters human life and promotes it.

The Bad, corollarily, is that which frustrates human life and smothers it. It is pain. It is that which stultifies human thought and human flourishing and prevents gain.

Thinking is the human method of survival. It is for this reason that humans are properly defined as the rational animal, and it is also for this reason that morality — true morality — is rooted not in God or gods or devils, but in the human quiddity: our rational faculty.

As a thing is defined by its identity, so humans are defined by their acts — which is to say, their actions.

Our actions are in turn shaped by our thoughts.

Your brain is the most powerful weapon in your arsenal. Nothing increases its strength like thinking. Cultivate, therefore, deliberate thought.

It is the greatest asset you've got.

***

Your life is largely a process of turning your interests into talents, which is done through a process of practice.

Talent is learned. It is cultivated.

Talent is not fated.

Your talents are rooted in the things you most enjoy doing.

It is in this sense that your passions are primarily willed.

Find your passions and grow them, and the more you do this, the more completely you'll be fulfilled.

***

If you want to go to college, go.

If your true desire in life requires something specialized or technical — like medicine or engineering or law — go.

By all means, this.

The point here is not to condemn college categorically, for condemnation sake.

The point here — the only point here — is that if you're going to college because that's what you've been told you should do, or because you've been told that you must go to college in order to have a more complete or successful life, do not go.

Do not go to college merely for lack of anything better.

If you don't yet know what you want to do, do not go.

Don't go back to college for that Bachelor's degree in sociology.

Don't go back to college to try and motivate yourself to write, or in an attempt to fill your time, or your head.

Cultivate your brain instead.

Read. Think. Blink. Drink.

Relax.

Be self-taught.

Learn to play the piano or piccolo or sax.

Read and think a lot.

There is no hurry — I assure you, there is no hurry.

I assure you, you need not worry. In fact, it is a good thing to not yet know what you want, because life is a gigantic canvas and there's so much with which to fill it, so much to do — have you not heard? So much, indeed, that choosing one thing at twenty or thirty or even forty is absurd.

College is far from the be-all-and-the-end-all. College is a lot of conformity and groupthink.

It can truly stunt your brain, every bit as much as lack of nourishment or food.

College is very often nothing more than pointless debt accrued.

***

Your desire to become the person you most want to become is ultimately the only thing you need.

In its elaboration, this will require a great deal — focus, discipline, practice — but the desire is the fundamental thing.

As long as there's a fundamental desire and it burns like a fire, there's no limit to anyone's achievement. You needn't be a savant. The desire to excel is the most important ingredient in becoming what you want.

***

"Life is an unceasing sequence of single actions, but the single action is by no means isolated," wrote Ludwig von Mises.

Your life is largely a process of transforming your interests into talents, which, in turn, comes about through a process of practice.

It is in this sense, I say again, that your passions are primarily willed, and not inborn or innate.

Even genius is willed. You *make* yourself great.

***

Life is work.

Jobs are healthy. Work is good. Work is good for the soul. Be happy in your work.

Nothing more fundamental than labor is required for the production of abundance and the good things that you want for your life.

Labor takes many forms.

Blue-collar jobs build character, as they build invaluable work habits that you'll never lose.

In her book *No Shame in My Game,* Katherine Newman points out what for many of us has been blindingly obvious for years: namely, that so-called low-skilled, blue-collar jobs, whether fast-food, waitressing, bartending, barista, custodial, clerking, so on, they require talents completely commensurate with, or even surpassing, white-collar work:

"Memory skills, inventory management, the ability to work with a diverse crowd of employees, and versatility in covering for co-workers when the demand increases," she writes.

Among many, many other skills, I add.

Servers, bartenders, baristas, expos, clerks, et cetera, must multitask and remember every bit as much as, for example, an ER doc.

That's one of the many reasons these jobs are good, and not something anybody should knock.

***

What do you value? Parties and thumbs-ups and reblogs and other time-killers, day and night? Or the active work of your body and brain?

Find work that you enjoy and embrace it. Become good at it. Become better. Pour your energy into your work like rain. Enjoy the motions of your body in concert with your brain.

He who's faithful in a little is faithful in a lot.

Everything you do, therefore, do it with all that you've got.

Wickedly Cool

Personality is personal style. It is nothing more and it is nothing less. The art of charisma is really the art of personality.

Which is why there are as many different ways to be charismatic as there are different styles of personality.

Personality is the sum total of one's many individual characteristics as they come together and create the person presented to the world.

Just as a thing is defined by its identity, so humans are defined by their acts, which are in turn defined by their thoughts.

Since we're each the shapers of our own thoughts — and *only* our own thoughts — we each have the power to change and to mold our own personality.

For this reason, charisma begins (and ends) in the brain.

Charisma is magnetism.

Magnetism, as the very word implies, is the power to attract.

People can be magnetic and charismatic in a multitude of different ways:

You don't, for instance, need to be extroverted to be charismatic.

You don't need to be gregarious or boisterous. Many of the most charismatic people you've ever seen are silent and strange.

Nor is physical beauty alone charismatic — or, at any rate, not in the full sense of the word:

Physical beauty attracts, esthetically, sexually, whathaveyou, but its power of attraction is limited, precisely because humans are conceptual: this means we think and ruminate and interact.

Magnetic qualities are ultimately qualities that demonstrate one's skills at living life as humans are designed to live it — which is to say, conceptually.

This is why contemplation is the highest occupation of the human species — because your personality and your behavior are a complex interplay of contemplation and action mixed. But it all begins in the brain.

Which, in general terms, is the reason that the most magnetic quality anyone can possess is the genuine happiness and the relaxed disposition that comes from a life that's been thought about and thus lived well, and then the genuine confidence which is the natural elaboration of that.

Perfection, however — and this is important — is *not* the determining factor in matters magnetic and charismatic:

Flaws, faults, foibles, and fuck-ups do not an uncharismatic person make.

How one *deals* with one's own flaws, faults, foibles, and fuck-ups is what's at primary issue.

Happiness is charismatic.

Understanding is charismatic.

Actual self-confidence is charismatic insofar as it discloses efficacy and worth.

Have you ever observed that you're at your best when you're doing something you really grasp?

Have you ever observed that you're at your most relaxed and comfortable when you're doing something you enjoy — i.e. something that you're genuinely confident in?

That state of mind is charismatic.

Have you, on the other hand, noticed that when you're put into a situation about which you know little or nothing and want no real part of, you feel diffident, timid, unhappy?

This is the opposite of charismatic.

The primary method of human survival is our rational capacity, because of which human survival isn't just physical but psychological.

That's why happiness is the goal.

The goal of life, then, is emotional. But the means of achieving it are not.

The means of achieving it are cognitive:

We must use our brains.

We must think.

Charisma stems from this uniquely human faculty.

Charisma comes from thinking.

So cultivate your power of thought.

Cultivate contemplation.

Contemplation, I repeat, is the highest occupation of the human species.

In the very decision to do this — and even more in the sincere follow-through — your charisma will EXPLODE.

Develop excellent eye contact.

Everyone knows that excellent eye contact is charismatic.

Everyone also knows that poor eye contact is a sign of diffidence and shyness.

Everyone knows that poor eye contact is a sign of distraction and a lack of interest.

Shifty eyes are fidgety eyes, and fidgety eyes do not attract but repel.

What most people don't know, however, is that excellent eye contact means relaxed eye contact. It's not some fierce, hyper-unwavering stare.

If you have trouble holding somebody's eyes, try looking instead at the multitude of different colors contained within her eyes. Make a scientific study of those colors.

Or:

Count their blinks, which has been demonstrated as an effective way to maintain proper eye contact.

Or:

Look at the eyelashes. Notice them. Count the individual strands, if you can.

Or:

Look only at the tip of the nose, which will appear to anyone whom you're talking with as if you're looking into her eyes.

Notice as well how you're physically feeling, and pay attention to that in an analytical way. This, believe it or not, will help with your eye contact.

Try this experiment:

Look at yourself in your phone-camera, or in your bathroom mirror. Then close your eyes and think of something in your life that's made you feel genuinely happy — happy to be alive. Concentrate on that thing. Actually put yourself back in the moment so that you're feeling it again.

Feel it for at least a half-minute.

Then open your eyes and observe what your eyes look like in that precise moment.

That's what charismatic eye contact looks like: relaxed and happy and soft.

Be still.

As you don't fidget with your eyes, so also don't fidget with your body.

Repose is *always* charismatic.

Repose is a hallmark of a relaxed disposition.

Develop and maintain proper posture and a purposeful walk.

Keep your back and shoulders straight, though not in an exaggerated or uncomfortable way.

Slouching isn't charismatic. It suggests listlessness and a certain lack of confidence.

Keep this good posture when you walk.

When you walk, walk purposefully but not overbearingly.

Be slow to speak and swift to hear.

And pause a beat or two before you begin speaking.

Slower speakers are almost universally regarded as more magnetic than those people who speak rapidly. Speak, therefore, more carefully, and speak also at the appropriate volume for the room or place you're in.

10 AUTHENTIC SIGNS OF INTELLIGENCE THAT CAN'T BE FAKED

Intelligence is your brain's capacity to deal with a wide range of thoughts and ideas.

Like most things, therefore, intelligence is a *process*.

It is not a static state.

It is not something you either have or don't.

Your brain is something you cultivate.

Intelligence stems fundamentally from thinking.

Thinking is a choice. It requires one essential thing: effort.

Thought is work. Thought is effort.

Thinking develops your brain. It increases your intellectual power and range.

Non-thought, corollarily, is something you can change.

You *become* brilliant.

You *learn* to be smart.

You are not afraid of new ideas because you know your brain can measure and weigh and test these new ideas — in the same way your brain can create new onomatopoeias.

A cultivated mind *is* an intelligent mind.

It is also beautiful and strange and rather difficult to find.

Thought is both the source and also the end result: it is the goal. It is the driving force.

It is an end in itself.

Intelligence is your ability to think.

This ability can be habituated and developed, or not, depending upon what you prefer to do with your time.

You know you're in the presence of a brain that's been cultivated when you see some of the following:

Fast, fluid handwriting that's legible.

There's a misbegotten notion that illegibility is a sign of a smart person, when in actuality it's the other way around:

People who write legibly want to be understood. Thus they make an effort to present themselves clearly, which takes brain power. Quick clear handwriting shows practice and patience, which in turn shows development.

Wit almost invariably signals that someone's mind has been cultivated:

Wit is mental sharpness. It is cognitive acuity. It is keenness.

Similarly — and for the same reasons — people who like to laugh, and who in turn like to make others laugh, are smart people.

A sharp sense of time and direction show brain power.

Why?

Because a sharp sense of time and direction indicate attention and focus.

The choice to focus or not is the seat of human thought.

The choice to pay attention is where it begins — and ends. It is the locus.

Smart people by definition are more curious.

They are thus more tolerant of ambiguity, just as they are also more tolerant of differences in others — grasping, as they do, what for many is the blindingly obvious:

The brain is a complicated place, and largely for this reason no two people are alike. This basic act of apprehension gives any person who performs it a more complex and more sophisticated mode of thinking.

Obsessive worry is an indicator of intelligence, because it discloses a racing mind that's never at rest but always thinking, always considering.

Which is why some of the greatest thinkers and innovators in world history were monomaniacal ruminators.

Smart people like to read for fun.

People who who take active pleasure in reading, rather than doing so out of duty and rather than reading purely for information, unquestionably have brains they've worked to cultivate — which means, among other things: "Avid readers have better memory function, communication skills, and focus."

Truly intelligent people like to often be alone.

Which doesn't necessarily mean they're introverted (although they can be), nor does it mean they don't like spending time among friends and with other people.

Rather, intelligent people prefer a lot of privacy and space, just as they prefer to pick and choose the time they spend among others, because they are independent and they value their independence, in part because it gives them time to *think*, as well as time to relax.

Smart people — genuinely smart people, as against the book-smart and the pedantic and all the other imposters — are autonomous and as such they have the authentic confidence that can only come from thought and the comprehension that thinking fosters.

Smart people are self-aware.

And *because* they are self-aware, smart people recognize their mistakes and failures, and they learn from them.

Self-awareness and insight into self is, incidentally, one of the few foolproof signs of intelligence.

People who can argue articulately and convincingly — and from many different angles — have, to that extent, clearly cultivated their brains:

Their minds through practice are able to move nimbly from one idea to another, like a long-legged spider skating upon the water.

Yet they are often slow to speak and swift to hear:

Genuinely smart people almost invariably consider what they're going to say before they say it. Their brain is honed in such a way that it's quicker than their mouth.

What, after all, does it mean to be smart?

It means to stylize your brain, like a work of art.

It means to cultivate your thoughts for as long as you're alive — cultivate your thoughts as if they're the plants of a living garden.

Cultivate them, yes, before your ideas, only partially thought through, ooze into dogma and then fully harden.

It means to observe the universe around you, as well as the one within: to introspect, as thoughtful people do.

It means to be intelligent, like you.

36:59.5

HOW TO PENETRATE PEOPLE'S BRAINS AS THOUGH YOU'RE TELEPATHIC

You're not telepathic, because telepathy doesn't exist, but you can learn to read people as *though* you are.

An ER doc whom I used to serve, who was a professional poker player as well and also a regular customer at this particular bar, once told me about a class he took on non-verbal tells and the science of body language — a class, he said, that he took to better hone his poker skills. It was taught by a retired FBI agent who for thirty years had specialized in this very thing.

The good doc told me that, somewhat to his surprise, while the class indeed benefitted his poker game — "inestimably," as he put it — it was how much it benefitted his medical practice that was the real bonus.

It taught him, in short, how to read his patients far more accurately.

He said that learning to observe and interpret non-verbal behavior altered his entire perspective and his practice in ways he could not have anticipated.

How?

Non-verbal behavior is ubiquitous and definite.

It is everywhere, and it is entirely reliable.

Once you learn even just a few of what the non-verbal expressions mean, you'll be astounded at what you can decode in the movements and micro-movements of everyone with whom you come in contact.

This is not pseudo-science, not quackery, and, in fact, the pseudo-science of so-called psychics rely in large measure on these very techniques.

Do you doubt it?

Consider this:

There are thousands upon thousands of movements and micro-movements humanly possible.

Ask yourself, then, are *any* of them telling?

Pursed lips?

A frown?

A wince?

A crooked smile?

Raised eyebrows?

Crossed arms?

Rubbing the back of the neck?

Open palms?

A crinkled nose?

A nostril flare?

A step backward?

A turn to the left?

Clenched fists?

Downcast eyes?

You see: even the most untrained person is able to decode certain non-verbals.

If you're still skeptical, try this:

Pull up a video clip of a movie or a television show you've never seen before and mute the volume.

Pay attention to what you're watching.

I assure you that if you pay attention you'll understand a great deal of what's going on merely from the movements and micro-movements of the actors. This is true even if it's a scene with only two people talking.

The brain, understand, is ultimately what controls all human behavior — whether that behavior is conscious or subconscious. This fact, which may sound obvious and even simplistic but which in actuality is quite profound, forms the underpinning of all non-verbal behavior.

The brain is the pilot. The body is the ship.

Watch people when they don't know they're being watched and what do you see?

You see a gallery of emotional activity.

Glance furtively, for example, at your spouse's face while you're driving to your in-laws' house for dinner — if, that is, you want to know how your spouse *actually* feels about your in-laws.

Concerning charisma, body language actually conveys more important information than words. There's little doubt about this.

No matter how powerful your verbal message, if your body language is wrong, you'll not have a charismatic presence.

On the other hand, good body language *in and of itself* is charismatic, apart from your verbal message.

"In the last 20 years, we've learned more about the communicative power of the human face than in the previous 20 millennia," wrote Daniel McNeill in his excellent book *The Face: A Natural History*.

With him here, I do not demur.

Learning the language of non-verbal communication is the real secret to penetrating people's brains.

How to Charm the Pants off Anyone Without Saying a Single Word

The following are five silent ways to charm the pants off anyone:

Smile sincerely but enigmatically

There are many different types of smiles.

There are fake smiles and there are cold smiles.

There are warm smiles and there are sly smiles.

There are guilty smiles and there are devilish smiles.

The principle that really matters here is to smile sincerely *but don't smile too quickly*.

To be sure, a large warm smile is *always* good, and you'll never go wrong with it.

A large warm smile that's slightly delayed — it's even better.

Why?

Because it makes people feel inundated with a smile that's meant exclusively for them.

Don't slouch

Stand up tall, lift your chin a little, and show the world your joy at the mere fact of being alive. Hold their eyes, yes, but hold them *softly*.

Hold their eyes

This is more important than you may realize. Maintain eye contact, as we previously discussed, but don't do it with a ferocious and fevered gaze.

Make your eye contact gentle and kind.

Remember: if at first you have trouble keeping eye contact, look instead at the tip of their nose, or, better yet, count their blinks, or scrutinize the multitudinous colors in their eyes.

When, at last, you look away, look away *slowly*.

People won't generally like you until they know you like them

That's a truism that holds up well.

Turn, therefore, fully toward a person and show the person that you are an open and friendly presence.

This in collaboration with your slow and flooding smile will put people at ease and showcase your likable personality.

Don't fidget

Don't paw at your face.

Don't wiggle your fingers.

Don't shift from foot to foot.

Don't nod too frequently.

Be *still*, for heaven sake.

Repose, remember, is always charismatic.

How to have People Dying to Hear What You'll Say Next

Don't speak.

Just listen.

Listen well.

Listen attentively.

Be the silent one.

Be the listener while everyone else is the talker.

Then, after everyone else has talked and talked, say something at last.

I guarantee — I absolutely guarantee you — that every single person will be *dying* to hear what you have to say.

How to Answer the Age-Old Question: What Do You Do?

"I ride motorcycles and make love to beautiful women," said the cool guy who worked on an assembly line in a glass factory, who loved women and who rode his motorcycle every chance he got. He was sitting at the bar answering a lovely lady who'd just asked him the age-old question.

His answer, I thought, was a good answer.

If, however, you're not in the mood to respond quite so obliquely or provocatively, always, at the very minimum, do this:

Give enough information about what you do that people can work with it. This is true, incidentally, no matter what your occupation.

If you're a waitress, for instance, say something like this:

"I'm a waitress. Do you eat french fries? If you do, the diner where I work serves french fries *so* good, they'll haunt you till they're gone.."

If you're a computer programmer, say something like:

"I write computer programs. I speak the language of code. It is a heavy load. Code is poetry. Do you speak it? It's okay if you don't. I speak semi-fluent English as well, and so we'll most likely still be able to communicate."

If you're a garbage hauler, you can say what I once heard an actual garbage-hauler say:

"I'd tell you, but you'd think it was total garbage. Okay. I'm a trash-hauler. It's an honest dollar."

The idea, whether you like my examples or not, is that no matter what you do — from the bluest of blue-collar jobs to the whitest of white-collar jobs — give your interlocutor something into which she can sink her teeth and *chew,* so that she might more easily regurgitate something back at you.

And never forget what Edgar Watson Howe once wrote:

"No man would listen to you talk if he didn't know it was his turn next."

How to Become a Freakishly Brilliant Small-Talker by Doing One Simple Thing

What is that one simple thing?

It is this:

Make people feel relaxed.

Small talk is not about content. It's about commiseration.

When you ask someone for the time and you're told how to build a clock, you'll not easily move forward.

When, upon the other hand, you ask for the time, and you're told "I don't know. The battery in my phone died — and it is a sad pass indeed when a man like me can't tell the time without his phone, don't you agree?" — you'll likely be put more at ease.

Think of conversation as a stroll. Think of it as a stroll that may or may not progress, depending upon your first few steps. Think of small talk as those first steps — and never forget that those steps consist only of one or two sentences.

The secret is to get in synch with whomever you're talking to.

Small talk, I repeat, isn't about content.

It's about mood.

Make your interlocutor comfortable, and you've gotten off on the correct foot.

How to Come Across as Diabolically Clever

"If you want to come across as devilishly clever," said the beautiful English professor, "all the degrees and all the accolades in the world pale in comparison to this one thing: learn to use 'who' and 'whom' correctly."

This, she said, will signal intelligence more than anything.

Failing that, I say, don't use "whom" at all but stick exclusively with "who."

Why?

Because nothing makes you sound less clever than misusing the word "whom."

"Our server," somebody once wrote, in a letter of complaint when I was managing-and-bartending, "whom never gave us her name …"

How will you ever take *that* letter seriously?

Cultivate wordplay:

Because your words are your thoughts verbalized, it is largely your words that make you clever. Seek, therefore, to describe things in a colorful and unorthodox manner:

"Hey, bartender, what's that mint-green bottle that stands out so clearly among the multicolored glass?"

You see?

That's good language.

Be persuasive:

How?

Learn facts and remember them.

Learn also to speak clearly and concisely, and always avoid jargon. This, without any doubt, is among the most persuasive and universal signs of cleverness there is:

The more clearly you present something, the more persuasive you are, and those who speak well speak briefly.

Learn quips, quotes, and anecdotes:

Learn many of them. Memorize them. Develop a deep well from which to draw so that you're not just recycling the same three or four or five and sounding like a broken record.

Don't use stale anecdotes:

It always delights a person when she or he hears a new story from an old friend.

Don't use stale cliches:

"My heart was beating like a drum, and when the moment finally came it cut like a knife."

Certain cliches, however, are colorful and even encouraged:

"Sharks? Well that's a different kettle of fish entirely...."

This sort of cliche you should embrace and enthusiastically use.

Never make a joke at someone else's expense for the sake of a laugh:

"Hey, baldie! Can you turn your head? The glare coming off you is blinding me."

It's tacky, it's amateurish, and, worst of all, it's fiercely unfunny.

Don't ever ask "What do you do?"

Instead, say something like:

"What in life brings you bliss?"

("God," she answered. "I spend virtually all my time at work, and so I'm afraid there's little time for bliss." At which point, almost magically, many conversational options have suddenly opened up before you, among which is the fact that you are now — only now — at liberty to ask what it is that occupies her time so.)

Don't use big or biggish words that you only partially understand but *do* cultivate a bigger vocabulary:

This is easier than you might think. Begin by learning fresher, less common words for standard things.

Instead of saying, for instance, "You look beautiful tonight," try:

"You look particularly radiant this evening."

Which, incidentally, I once heard a very kind and clever fellow say to a middle-age woman he knew, though only a little, who had just sat down next to him at the bar, and this woman, I swear to you, was walking on sunshine all night long from that one compliment alone.

Observe clever people and try to understand precisely what you find clever about them — and then copy that principle.

The most important thing of all:

Believe that you can become more clever.

Because you can.

Because it's not how smart or clever you *are*.

It's how smart and clever you *want* to be.

Lynchpin

For you, the secret was never a secret, quite, because for you it always seemed natural — not necessarily easy, of course, but obvious, and obviously right.

It never mystified you, perhaps because you learned long ago that your body is a ship, your brain the pilot at the tip.

Which is why everything you ever decided to do you learned to do with skill, having discovered that in matters such as these the decisive factor is the human will.

You discovered that the secret key to the lock of life is nothing more — or less — than developing a durable purpose around which to arrange all the other things in your life, and against which all other things are measured and weighed.

This, in any case, is what you conveyed.

A central purpose, as you say, is the unifying factor that molds together the human clay and integrates all the other factors in your life, year-to-year, month-to-month, day-to-day. So that to be in control of your own life, you must *build* this fundamental purpose, and then not let it go.

But why is this so?

Because purpose forms the base and at the same time creates a kind of pyramid, the stones of which are your other desires, arranged in order of importance. This, in turn, spares you any number of internal clashes and strife. This great pyramid is your life.

The central purpose that forms its base allows you to enjoy existence more abundantly, and on the widest conceivable scale.

You, having discovered this long ago, could never after that truly go too far astray, or too disastrously fail.

All the rest fell naturally into place.

It's one reason people argue about the liveliness of your eyes. It's why they discuss the ineffable quality of your face.

She was always a little reckless, they say, a reckless shooter, a long-shot, a shoot-from-the-hipper, but despite her wild misses always, deep down, believed she could be a star. There's a certain languorous confidence about her (they say) a certain laid-back quality that's fascinating, yes, but somehow it seems taken a little far.

It makes her remote and solitary, like a star.

Still, she's kind and well-spoken and oddly charismatic, if rather fanatic, who never cared to hunt with the horde — indeed, never hunted at all — but chose instead to focus first upon the work, whatever it was (night-audit, waitress, secretary, clerk), not the party boys or the alcohol-fueled life.

Nor, indeed, was there ever in you the all-consuming drive to be somebody's girlfriend, or mistress, or wife.

Work is healthy, you say, jobs are good for the soul. Work provides an outlet for creativity and expression. Life is work. Life is purposeful effort. It is an unceasing sequence of individual actions. Productive work is for this reason not meant to be a perfunctory performance, or jail sentence. It's just the opposite: it's a creative act, an act that's nourishing.

Productive effort is the *sine-qua-non* of human happiness and flourishing.

It's your continual progress forward, one step to another, one step at a time, one achievement to another, always upward and always guided by the continual expansion of your mind, your knowledge, your inexhaustible versatility and limitless ingenuity.

Be happy in your work.

Do you at any time reach a point when it's too late to find a purpose, ever?

No, you say, never.

Are You Fascinating?

Well, are you, punk?

Or are you boring as hell?

How, furthermore, can you tell?

How can you tell if you're an inveterate bore, or if you're just in a kind of long-term funk?

Much of what we hear about commanding attention and the power to fascinate is theoretical and abstract, a sort of psychological jargon: fascination triggers, hotspots, personality tests and the like.

Let us, for once, get concrete.

Here are seven differences between the fascinating person and the boring piece of meat:

68

Fascinating people have many activities they enjoy and become good at, which gives them a greater wealth of material to mine

Boring people have one or perhaps two.

Diversify, therefore, your activity portfolio, and through this one thing alone, you'll have come a long way in becoming irresistibly fascinating.

Fascinating people communicate what most others can't — or communicate it in ways most others don't.

Words, contrary to popular belief, are not primarily for communicating — which is their secondary function. Their primary function is for clarity of thought.

Before one can communicate clearly, one must have something to communicate clearly.

Language brings about this process.

The desire for clarity presupposes the desire to be understood, and this is why the ability to communicate clearly — in writing or in speech — is one of the surest signs of intelligence there is.

And intelligence, as you know, is always fascinating.

Remember also: those who speak well speak briefly.

Fascinating people aren't afraid to try new things — which means:

They're not only willing to break out of their comfort zone but also motivated to do so. Why?

Because they know that comfort breeds complacency.

Interesting people, understand, are, to one degree or another, adventurous. They like to get out and explore.

Life is largely an adventure — provided you treat it as such.

Fascinating people are *au courant.*

They keep up-to-date on at least some news.

Which is why as a bartender you often find yourself charmed by those customers who have a certain knowledge of pop culture: because this, too, shows that an effort is being made to stay informed.

Thus:

Fascinating people are knowledgable.

Boring people are poorly informed — and so they're unable to hold up their end of the conversation.

Being poorly informed, let it be noted, is entirely within each person's control.

The better you're informed, the more you have to talk about.

The more you have to talk about, the more fascinating you are.

Which is not to imply that fascinating people blast through one conversational subject after another.

It means, rather, that the deeper down your knowledge goes, the greater is your conversational *pow-uh*.

Fascinating people don't conform

Independent thinking is non-conformity.

Conformity is about as boring and banal as it gets.

Fascinating people have the confidence to think for themselves.

Boring people do not.

Fascinating people like variety.

Boring people prefer the same old.

Conformity is the same old.

It is also the opposite of courage. It takes courage to respond to non-thought — which is to say, conformity — just as it takes courage to break away from the pack.

It takes courage to think for oneself.

If you're one of these rare courageous people, the world will be riveted by you.

Fascinating people are happy and driven and disciplined.

Boring people are passive.

Discipline is habit, and habit is a choice.

This is precisely why no one is fated to be boring — not even close.

How, then, does one go about expunging inveterate vapidity?

Studies show that you can bore people in two fundamental ways: both in *what* you say and in *how* you say it.

Being boring, in other words, can be a matter of style or a matter of subject. Combine those two things into one and it's downright deadly.

The qualities that make someone fascinating, or beguiling, or hypnotizing, or mesmerizing are — and this is important — a side-effect. They are a by-product: a by-product of a life lived well, a life lived interestingly.

The real insight into the power of fascination is this:

The fascinating person is not living her life to *be* fascinating: she's living her life in a way that cultivates her living potential, and that's why age cannot wither her, nor custom stale her infinite variety.

Make no mistake, there are in the universe an infinite variety of fascinating things upon which you may fix your attention.

To be fascinating, therefore, you must come to recognize life as the adventure it is, and you must then proceed accordingly.

You must crave new experiences and desire a deeper understanding of the world.

Decide what you want and figure out how to get it.

Boring people don't have big dreams. They actually believe it when they're told, as we all are at one time or another, that they probably can't do it.

Fascinating people, upon the other hand, believe no such thing.

Fascinating people shoot for the stars — and often reach them. If they don't reach them, they become incontrovertibly more fascinating just in their singleminded striving.

Fascinating people picture their lives as they want their lives to be, and then they focus their energy on shaping their lives in that way.

Don't let others decide your future for you. Don't give people that kind of control over you. This is not only *not* fascinating: it's fatal.

Be the master of your own fate. Be the captain of your own soul.

Because, in the final analysis, fascinating people are the shapers of their own soul.

And that is why they seem to others not fractured but whole.

How to be Unforgettable

Most people are boring. Not you.

Why?

Because you broke away from the pack a long time ago. You're a different breed — a dog of a different color.

You cultivated the black art of individuality, learned the art of personality. You became brilliant. People argue about your modesty.

She does things differently, they say, she's heterodox, self-contained, haunting the higher eminences of thought, hard-worker, school-leaver, reposed, self-taught.

Like all of us, she's a tightly packed pod of living potential, but she's EXPLODING: a life-giving force, a mustard seed.

She's never in need.

She has the common touch. Yet, somehow, she remains pure and remote and above the fray.

She has a certain way.

She's silent. She's sensible.

She's sane.

She's generous.

She's still.

She's esoteric.

She's inquisitive.

She's relevant.

She's independent.

She knows that self-development is the aim of life and that self-control is the basis of character.

She's happy.

She's not sloppy.

It takes a certain kind of work to be boring, whereas in order to be interesting it's ... what?

It's mostly a question of habit — and the true secret of habit, as everyone knows, is the insight that habit is discipline and that your habits are what you choose them to be.

Your life is your values.

Your values are what you most enjoy doing.

In this sense, your values are your habits.

How do you become unforgettable?

1. Cultivate your desire for knowledge

Work to want it more. Knowledge is at home in any public house, coffee-shop, diner, saloon, or bar.

Strive to become the unstoppable learning beast of unslakable thirst that you know you are.

How?

By generalizing. Specialize, yes, that too, but read a little about a lot — or, if you don't like to read, listen.

Take a course. Attend a lecture. Plug into a podcast. Take in a play.

Most importantly: seek to integrate the new things you learn into the full body of your existing knowledge. In this way, your web of learning will become interconnected, contextual, hierarchical, sweeping.

2. Learn to listen in a charismatic way

You heard me right. (Or did you?)

People love to hear themselves talk. Not you. You're far too interesting for that. You're far too self-contained.

Attentive listening is an infallible hallmark of magnetism and manners — which two things go together like whiskey and wieners.

By being an excellent listener, slow to speak and swift to hear, you'll go far in developing a kind of irresistible fascination.

Brilliant listeners focus sincerely on what the other person is saying.

They never participate in a conversation with the mindset that they'll listen only until it's their turn to talk.

If the whole time you're listening, you're thinking about what you're going to say next, it will show on your face like food in one's beard.

If you're fidgety, this, too, will show invariably.

In your patience possess ye your souls.

Patience and presence are signals of extraordinary listeners.

Good listeners do this:

Pause before they respond.

Never interrupt.

Allow in total silence people to interrupt them.

3. Become a passionate storyteller

How?

Simple:

Create stories around subjects that you're truly passionate about.

If the subject of your story is something you're genuinely interested in, your personality will BLAST through, and you'll be exposed as the ferocious creative force of insatiable appetite that you know you are.

Those who speak well speak briefly.

And remember:

Talent is meaningless.

There's not even really any such thing as talent.

Ambition is everything.

The truth is that the overwhelming majority of successful people aren't particularly gifted or educated or blessed. Rather, they become successful, in any given endeavor, because they will it.

How to be the Smartest Person in the Bar

You can spot her from a mile away, the smartest person in the bar — or, if not quite from a mile, nonetheless from very far.

She doesn't necessarily think of herself as smart.

Still, her brain is carefully crafted — self-crafted and stylized — like a work of art.

Her eyes are alert and bright and lively. They twinkle.

She's relaxed and polite, with a well-modulated voice that speaks to you in the appropriate tone.

Her smile glows like expensive stone.

You do not quickly forget that smile.

She walks purposefully, and yet not aggressively, or with an overbearing style.

She has a sense of humor.

You can see that she knows there's a kind of dignity in loneliness. She doesn't go out of the way to seek friends or groups or any kind of crowd.

In general she prefers quiet to loud.

She gives and receives compliments gracefully, can be strong and assertive, quick to stick up for herself, but she can also speak of her shortcomings and accomplishments with an equal ease which you envy.

When communication or clarification is called for, she's never dismissive or inexplicably silent — never, of course, in any way aggressive or violent.

What's her trick?

What's the secret?

The secret is this:

First, develop a total disregard for where you think your abilities end.

Aim beyond what you believe you're capable of.

Do things you think you're not able to do.

Nothing is impossible, in this regard. The will to believe is the most important ingredient in becoming what you want.

The discipline to follow through is next. It is also the most difficult.

Why?

Why most difficult?

Because it requires hour-after-hour, day-after-day practice.

It requires diligence.

Second — unless you're in a technical discipline like medicine or mechanical engineering — drop out of college *immediately*.

College stifles creativity, stunts the mind.

College is conformity.

The cost of conformity is colossal.

Individuality, on the other hand, is a prerequisite of genius.

Genius is the cultivation of your living potential.

The deeper your cultivation, the deeper your genius.

Cultivate, therefore, a durable purpose (not food, not drink, not cigars, or other ephemeral things) around which you can construct your life.

Passion is largely willed: the more you do something, the deeper your understanding of it grows, so that after time your passion for that thing develops and spreads like a gorgeous soft surge of water-ripples.

Whatsoever thy hand findest to do, do it with all thy might.

Third, be observant.

Pay attention.

Attention is the seat of human will: the fundamental choice we face, all day, everyday, is the choice to pay attention or not.

What, after all, does it mean to be smart?

It means to self-stylize your brain, like a work of art.

It means to observe the universe around you, as well as the one within: to introspect, as thoughtful people do.

It means to be intelligent, like you.

Intelligence is your mental capacity to deal with a wide range of thoughts and ideas.

That's why it never mattered to you when you were voted least likely to succeed — why it never fazed you when they called you a misfit, a malcontent, alienate, disaffiliate, deviant, recalcitrant. And it's why your natural-born predilections and proclivities and predispositions are and always have been irrelevant: because intelligence is an *acquired* skill.

It must be developed by each person's own desire and activated by each person's will.

It must be habituated and automated by each person's own mind.

Which is why it's quite rare and beautiful, and rather difficult to find.

This, incidentally, is true for both children and adults: the cultivation of intelligence requires effort — or, to put the same point in a slightly different way: thinking is an act of choice.

Thought requires work.

Whereas to be stoopid is relatively simple: all you have to do, in essence, is do nothing. If you do nothing, stoopid will naturally occur.

Being smart, however, requires a different sort of action.

It's not passive.

On the contrary, thinking is an entirely active process the undertaking of which is, when you consider it at all, massive.

She's intelligent, yes, but in a highly unorthodox way (they say) hard to pinpoint why: bookish but not book-smart, introspective, certainly, and everything she does — yes, *everything* — she does with all her heart.

101 Things to do Instead of College

The following list is by no means exhaustive — you can brainstorm hundreds more — and most, though not all, involve starting a business or teaching (online, or brick-and-mortar, or both) the doing of which, thanks largely to the internet, has never been easier:

Don't, however, do what I've done a thousand times, or more:

Don't pick too many things, so that you end up doing none.

Pick one.

Pick two at most.

Take time to decide on something. Make a definite commitment — not for life (unless you want) but for a few months. Devote time to it every day. Learn it. Practice it.

***

1. Learn wood-working, carpentry

2. Become a stonemason

3. Learn to landscape

4. Write books and publish them on Amazon (I can help — hit me up)

5. Learn a language and teach it online. There is a demand. Learn more languages.

6. Become an apprentice — electrician, bricklayer, carpenter, plumber. The work is good, and the money is great.

7. Start your own podcast about something that interests you, whether it be history or poetry or

permaculture or anything. Build your audience and I promise you the money will follow

8. Become a YouTube superstar

9. Work construction

10. Work road construction

11. Bartend (the money is good)

12. Waitress or barista (the money is good)

13. Get your CDL and drive a truck (the money is good)

14. Start a knife-sharpening business — or, better yet, learn to make knives and sell them

15. Educate yourself and become good at something — anything: kite-making, fly-tying, photography, writing — and teach courses, by book, video, podcast, live, or all of the above. You need not be an expert to teach.

16. Master yoga and teach it

17. Make crafts and art and set up an Etsy shop

18. Learn to fight — Ju Jitsu, boxing, Krav Maga, Kung Fu — and teach it

19. Make people laugh and do it on YouTube, or via podcast

20. Start a small farm

21. Start a small hydroponic or organic farm (the demand has never been greater)

22. Teach farming

23. Learn forestry

24. Become a card-dealer

25. Learn locksmithing (always hiring)

26. Tow-truck driver (always hiring)

27. Learn to code (always a demand for that skill)

28. Become a handyman, or start your own window-washing business

29. Read books and teach these books: do books-synopsis podcast (it's in high demand with college students)

30. Make movies

31. Direct documentaries

32. Start a small newsletter and grow it

33. Start a website that's about something you love — knitting, tea, coffee, vegan, paleo — and grow that website.

34. Become a butcher

35. Become a pot grower

36. Start your own floor-cleaning business

37. Start a dog-walking business

38. Write jingles and songs and sell your services or become a YouTube superstar

39. Sell merchandise through a Facebook fan page

40. Sell merchandise through an Instagram fan page

41. Sell merchandise through a Pinterest page

42. Sell merchandise through the massive Twitter following you've built

43. Start a radio show, via podcast, wherein you interview experts in your chosen topic (experts are always looking for a platform to showcase their books or their knowledge or both)

44. Sell things on eBay

45. Sell things on Craigslist

46. Volunteer at a hospital

47. Work as a paralegal

48. Write scripts

49. Audition on Broadway for a full year

50. Become a real-estate agent

51. Become a party-planner

52. Start your own cleaning business

53. Sell dildos and other sex toys

54. Become a sommelier

55. Read a book a week

56. Cultivate your memory and teach memory

57. Copy verbatim in long-hand an entire book you love, and you'll be amazed at how much you learn about the craft of writing. This is is the method by which Benjamin Franklin, among others, taught himself to write

58. Study what interests you. Get hold of something that bothers you and solve the problem — and then write about it, broadcast it, podcast it

59. Develop an app (Instagram and SnapChat made people into millionaires or billionaires)

60. Get on the speaking circuit and give talks on subjects about which you're passionate (places are always looking for speakers, and they pay well)

61. Learn to mine, and go in search of gold (the mountains are virtually untapped, all enviro propaganda to the contrary notwithstanding)

62. Consult in your area of expertise

63. Become an auto mechanic

64. Become an airplane mechanic

65. Learn to fly helicopters

66. Work in the oil fields (great money, honest work)

67. Become an esthetician

68. Become a tattoo artist

69. Become a henna artist

70. Teach people how to paint

71. Teach people how to sculpt

72. Master a popular video game and become a YouTube superstar (extraordinarily popular subject, and this demographic spends money)

73. Learn to barber, or become a hair stylist

74. Teach Photoshop or Lightbox (always in demand)

75. Start a thrift store

76. Hold weekly yard sales or garage sales (you'd be surprised the money you can make)

77. Learn to write good sales copy, and you'll never have to worry about money again, because good copywriters are sought after

78. Learn magic and perform it

79. Become a heavy equipment operator

80. Drive for Lyft or Uber

81. Start your own clean-up-after-construction-crew business

82. Learn to be a house-painter

83. Learn to be a glass glazier

84. Learn to bake delicious pies and you'll never have to worry about money again

85. Learn ventriloquism and perform it on YouTube and in real-life

86. Learn to weld

87. Teach your video-audio skills (there's always a demand for this)

88. Teach photography

89. Administrate other people's social media

90. Become a repo man or woman (I've done this one: great money, slightly dangerous)

91. Become a private detective (I've also done this one, and it can be great money as well)

92. Become a process server

93. Become a fishing or hunting guide

94. Learn to make paper and candles and teach people (there's a demand for this)

95. Become an EMT/Paramedic

96. Auto sales

97. Car detailer and mobile car-cleaning business

98. Fix computers (mobile business)

99. Become a florist or a horticulturist

100. Do you like blood? Become a phlebotomist

101. Teach dance, online and off

***

Here's the most important thing — the secret to changing the world:

Learn to sell your skills.

You don't have to be an expert. You just have to know more about a given thing than other people know about that thing.

Have you, for instance, spent time in the insurance industry?

Your insights, I guarantee you, will be invaluable to young people wanting to break into that industry.

Sell your insights.

The Art of Independent Thinking

Individualism is the act of thinking for yourself. It's rooted in the most fundamental choice you've got: the choice to pay attention or not.

There are approximately one thousand arguments against individualism — and every single one of them, without exception, is predicated upon a fraudulent premise.

That human beings are, for instance, essentially social doesn't negate or nullify our individualistic nature.

True individualism is not "rugged." The next time you hear that, dismiss it immediately for exactly what it is: a canard, if ever there was one.

Karl Marx saw humanity as an "organic whole," and all the Neo-Marxists like to use that phrase, pointing out simultaneously the obvious fact that "most humans grow up in families and live in societies." All of which misses the point and does not render individualism void:

Individualism does not mean atomism.

Neither does it mean that humans are anti-social by nature.

Nor does individualism necessarily embrace self-destructive hedonism, or moral subjectivism, or moral relativism, or fleeting range-of-the-moment pleasures that are too short-sighted to consider long-term consequences — or any of the other adversary ethics that nullify human happiness over a lifespan.

Ultimately, the thing that grounds individualism in fact is that no one person can think for another:

Only the individual reasons.

Only the individual thinks.

Thought is the fundamental act of human will.

When you distill it down to its essence, the decision to pay attention or not is the choice that determines all your other choices because it's what determines your thoughts.

For this reason it's not an exaggeration to say that the locus of free will is in the choice to pay attention or not.

We are each defined by our actions, but our actions are defined by our thoughts.

The choice to focus your attention is the spark that shapes and determines everything else because that choice is what shapes your thinking patterns.

Thinking is the uniquely human method of survival.

Thinking is reasoning.

Reasoning is the power of the human brain to form connections and make distinctions — which is to say: reason is the human capacity to discover the *identity* of things.

It is the process of learning the nature of reality. It is the process of learning what things are.

Recognizing this will take you far.

Reason is choice, said John Milton.

This insight — what it implies — is ultimately the thing that embeds individualism in fact.

Societies, communities, tribes, bands, and so forth — all are composed of individuals. But each of those individuals must perform alone, in the privacy of their own minds, the fundamental thing that shapes every subsequent thing:

Each individual must choose to focus the brain and pay attention, or not.

That is where the art of individualism begins, and ends. It is the most essential choice you've got.

What is Friendship?

The beautiful Japanese word *kenzoku* connotes a chemistry or a bond sourced in similarity of spirit.

It suggests the sharing of certain fundamental values.

It is in this sense that our most profound connections come from our power of choice — not birth or blood — because our values are chosen and developed by each one of us individually.

Friendship, in a very real sense, comes from our capacity to value.

Valuing is an individual choice. It stems from your thoughts.

Our values are our passions.

Our passions are largely willed.

Those who value things most deeply, feel love most deeply.

Friendship is a spectrum: there are different degrees, types, and depths. And yet they all have one thing in common:

They're all founded upon esteem and affection for the other person.

Friendship is reciprocal.

The friends whom you feel the most affection for are the friends who reflect your deepest values.

You needn't even have very much in common with your closest friends: provided you're likeminded in certain *fundamental* things — this, more than anything, will bond you at the most fundamental level.

Love is in this way mirror-like: it reflects those values you yourself hold most dear.

"Natural love is nothing more than the fundamental inclination which is stamped upon every being by the Author of nature."

Said Thomas Aquinas.

Like his teacher Aristotle, Aquinas believed that the highest love was friendship.

Both, however, believed that friendship was just a precursor to understanding the love that is, in Aquinas's words, *caritas*.

One of the first questions Aquinas poses in his tract on caritas is whether it equals friendship. He answers this way:

*According to Aristotle (**Ethics VIII, 4**) not all love has the character of friendship, but only that love which goes with wishing well, namely when we so love another as to will what is good for him. For if we do not will what is good to the things we love but rather, we will their good for ourselves, as we are said to love wine, a horse or the like, then that is not* *love of friendship but a love of desire. For it would be foolish to say that someone has friendship with wine or a horse.*

But benevolence alone does not suffice to constitute friendship; it also requires a certain mutual loving, because a friend is friendly to his friend. But such mutual benevolence is based on something shared in common.

Both also believed that love is *active.*

Thus, when there ceases to be reciprocity, there ceases to be love.

When there ceases to be an active and passionate mind, there ceases to be values.

When there ceases to be values, the capacity for friendship is proportionately diminished.

Love and friendship are both life-affirming and also life-giving: they are an interplay of mirror-like reflection and exchange. They both begin with the individual's capacity to value.

Life is largely a process of valuing.

And valuing begins — and ends — in the individual mind.

Laissez-Nous Faire

Laissez faire is first and foremost a beautiful notion:

Leave the world alone. It manages itself.

In many ways this idea is the very seat of human civilization.

The term is pronounced **lay-say-FAIR** and derives its present-day meaning from Vincent de Gournay's half-forgotten codification:

Laissez-faire et laissez-passer, le monde va de lui même.

"Let it be and let goods pass: the world goes by itself."

People who believe in total, unadulterated laissez faire, as I do, believe that society contains within it the capacity for ordering and managing its own path of development.

This includes ecosystems of every stripe and variety, which are clearly best managed by a system of full private property rights, and not centralized planning committees or an elite bureau who determine everything for the rest of us.

It follows thus that people should enjoy the liberty to manage their own lives, associate as they please, exchange with anyone and everyone, which includes — and please listen closely — *owning and accumulating property and otherwise being unencumbered even when one grows very wealthy.*

For all the lip-service they pay anarchism, the egalitarians, the communitarians, the agrarians, and all other similarly-minded groups, they simply do not tolerate hierarchy, neither in wealth-and-property accumulation, nor in employment structure — blanking out, of course, the incontrovertible fact that human beings possess varying degrees of motivation and ambition: the two greatest factors in "inequality and privilege."

It is for this reason that implementing egalitarianism in any form requires the diametric opposite of laissez faire: it requires force.

Laissez faire asks only this: that you leave others alone.

Laissez faire is deeply connected with the concept of individual rights.

Laissez faire states that your rights, my rights, everyone's rights stop where another's begin.

There are, in the present day, two main alternatives to laissez faire, neither of which is more convincing than the other:

There is the so-called Left, which, to speak generally, believes that if we let the economic sphere be free, the world will collapse. The Left then hypothesizes all manner of disaster that will befall humankind without government control.

And then there is the so-called Right, which is every bit as misbegotten, convinced as it is that state control must happen in, for instance, your bedroom, or the world will collapse into debauchery and crime and war.

Laissez faire rejects both views — for (semi) obvious reasons:

"The harmony of interests," as Claude Frédéric Bastiat called it, which make up the social order, and the fact that human freedom is a birthright.

Laissez faire is the view that the artists and the creators, the merchants and the business-people, the philanthropists and the farmers, the entrepreneurs and property-owners — all, in short, should be left alone.

It is the view that everyone, regardless of race, sex, sexual orientation, color, class, or creed, possesses the inalienable right to her own life and property — and *only* her own life and property — and this is the only way for all humans to live freely.

How to Drop Out of School, Fire Your Boss, & Change the World

A single idea has the power to change the world, forever and for the better.

Never doubt that.

People who change the world have this one thing in common: an unrelenting drive — not so much to change the world, but to perform the task they set out to do.

Because you needn't live your life as anyone else wants or expects you to live it.

Your life is your own.

"Once in a while it really hits people that they don't have to experience the world in the way they have been told to," said Alan Keightley.

115

Like the mysterious man who, on June 4th, 1989, stood bravely before a column of tanks after the Chinese military had violently quashed protests in Tiananmen Square, killing thousands of students. This man — Tank Man, as he's now known — impeded the tanks, and his image and act, captured on camera and broadcast worldwide, will never be forgotten. It changed the world.

Like the anonymous woman who, at twenty-six-years-old, shortly after her husband died, decided it was as good a time as any to shape some small section of the world in her own image and likeness — and proceeded then to write a strange, small newsletter, which developed a following so large that her ideas soon began to swell and spread all throughout the country and then the world.

Like Arianna Huffington.

Like Matt Drudge.

Like Markos Moulitsas.

Like Michelle Malkin.

Like Frederick Douglas.

Like Napoleon Hill.

Like Stephen Covey.

Like Martin Luther King.

Like Rosa Parks.

Like thousands upon thousands of others.

As I said in the beginning:

You *must* start thinking of your passions and your dreams as your profession — your life-force, your reason for living.

Start today.

Start now.

You just have to do it.

It's do or die:

Life is do or die.

So go and do.

And to hell with swords and garter — and anything else that strangles the creative beastie so desperately yearning to hatch open and take shape inside of you.

Made in the USA
Columbia, SC
03 June 2018